STRESSED
OUT
STUDENTS
GUIDE
TO
HANDLING
PEER
PRESSURE

STRESSED OUT STUDENTS STUDENTS GUIDE TO HANDLING PEER PRESSURE

Series Editor
Lisa Medoff, Ph.D.

Published by Kaplan Publishing, a division of Kaplan, Inc.
1 Liberty Plaza, 24th Floor
New York, NY 10006

Printed in the United States of America

First printing: 2008
10 9 8 7 6 5 4 3 2 1

SOS: Stressed Out Students' Guide to Handling Peer Pressure
ISBN-13: 978-1-4277-9807-7

Kaplan Publishing books are available at special quantity discounts to use for sales promotions, employee premiums, or educational purposes. Please email our Special Sales Department to order or for more information at kaplanpublishing@kaplan.com, or write to Kaplan Publishing, 1 Liberty Plaza, 24th Floor, New York, NY 10006.

Got stress?

**Learn how to overcome the stress of
peer pressure.**

**Stories and real-life advice told *by*
teens *for* teens to help cope with
stress—for students and parents alike.**

ABOUT THE SERIES EDITOR

Lisa Medoff holds a B.A in psychology from Rice University, an M.S.Ed. in school counseling from the University of Pennsylvania, and a Ph.D. in child and adolescent development from Stanford University.

For the past ten years, Lisa has been working with middle and high school students who have learning disabilities and emotional disorders. In this job, Lisa consults with both families and schools to help them provide the optimal school and home environments for their children with special needs.

She has taught child & adolescent development and psychology courses to both undergraduates and teacher credential candidates at Stanford University, Santa Clara University and San Jose State University.

Lisa works with the non-profit Cleo Eulau Center of Palo Alto, providing consulting services and teacher education workshops for elementary school teachers in a high-risk school district. She is also the author of a weekly child psychology column for the website Education.com.

CONTENTS

CONTENTS

CONTENTS

CONTENTS

CONTENTS

CONTENTS

CHAPTER 12: Fighting Off What's Fighting You: Stress Management

INTRODUCTION

I can't believe I did that. That so wasn't me. I would be totally humili-ated if my girlfriend ever found out. I hope no one caught that little incident on their cell phone and posted it online. I would give anything if I could just go back one hour and do it all over again. I never would have done that if it weren't for him. I wish I had said something at the begin-ning to stop it from happening before it was too late.

Have any of these thoughts ever run through your mind? If so, you're not alone. We all do things we're not proud of. What's weird is that we usually do these things when we're with our friends. We do crazy stuff around them that we would never do if we were alone or with our fami-lies. Why is that? Usually it's because we're afraid. We're afraid that others will laugh at us. Call us names. Make fun of us. Stop inviting us to their parties. Ignore us.

Being around our friends can hurt our judgment because all of these fears start to take over our brains. They drain us of our confidence and strength. Even if we know that what we're doing is wrong, we may not

INTRODUCTION

think that it's worth it to stand up for ourselves, or for others. We're so afraid that our friends (or the people that we want to be our friends) will look down on us or reject us.

All of the adults in your life tell you not to worry about what others think. They tell you to just do your own thing, but it's not that simple, is it? Adults love to worry about peer pressure. But they seem to worry about it only when you're doing something they don't want to you do, right? They don't get upset with you when you get good grades like your friends, do they? They only get worried when you want to do all the fun and exciting stuff that your friends are doing. It's annoying, I know. But cut your parents and teachers just a little bit of slack. They are probably remembering the days when they were your age, and they felt pressured to do something that they later regretted. They are trying to spare you the bad feelings they had to live with. Opportunities they missed out on. People they hurt that they still feel guilty about. We study history in order to avoid repeating the mistakes of the past, so consider learning a history lesson from the adults that you know. Attempt to resist peer

INTRODUCTION

pressure by taking some time to really think about the all decisions that you have to make.

It's not a bad thing to look to your friends to see if what you are doing is right, acceptable, or cool. We all do that, even adults. Nobody wants to be laughed at (except comedians), so we watch others to make sure our clothes are in style and our behavior is appropriate for the situation. If people didn't conform and follow what others are doing to some degree, things would get pretty wild and confusing out there. We could never be sure if we understood exactly what someone else meant. We would be worried every second of the day about looking silly or offending others. And just think about driving in a world where everyone followed his or her own traffic rules.

However, it is never smart to blindly accept what others do or say. And yes, you should remember that idea the next time your teacher is lecturing (but remember to be polite about it — I don't want you sitting in detention for the next few weeks because of me). Some of the students

INTRODUCTION

that I respect the most are the ones who are brave enough to challenge me when I am lecturing. I know they're listening, and I know they're thinking. Sometimes I even end up changing my point of view a little bit (or a lot!) because my students have made me see something in a different way that I had never even considered. Civil rights revolutions and breakthroughs in technology come about because someone had the guts to say, "Hey, why do we have to do things like this?"

So question what others tell you. Ask why. Figure out if there is information that you're not getting, or if there is another way of looking at the situation. Make your friends do a little work to earn your approval. Who says that their opinion is anymore worthwhile or correct than yours? Very bad things happen in societies where people do not question their leaders, for expample, the deaths of millions of people. I'm not saying that you smoking a cigarette because your friend teased you into doing it is the same thing as mass genocide, but the underlying ideas are not all that different.

INTRODUCTION

Be suspicious of anyone who tries to pressure you into doing anything. He or she does not necessarily know what is right or cool. Think about it. If you know you have the right answer in class, do you need to ask your friends what they think before you raise your hand? If you know that new shirt looks amazing on you, do you need to ask someone else's opinion before you wear it to school? No, you don't. You have the confidence to go ahead and say the answer or wear the shirt. When someone else is trying to force you to follow him, it's usually because deep down, he's not sure that he's doing the right thing. He needs you to do it, too, so he can feel better about himself. Why should you risk your reputation, safety, or future just to make someone else feel good?

What your friends want you to do might not seem all that crazy. Turn on the television or the computer, and what do you see? Celebrities doing really outrageous things. Driving drunk. Getting messed up on drugs. Screaming racial slurs. Crazy sex tapes. Lying. Wearing ridiculous clothes just because they cost $10,000 (per leg). Then they apologize, go to rehab, and everything is okay again. So why shouldn't you be able

INTRODUCTION

to have a little bit of fun like those celebrities? Everything always turns out okay for them, doesn't it? Well, why do you think that is? They have a manager, a publicist, a lawyer, an agent, a personal relations rep, and hundreds of other people who run around behind the scenes making sure that everything turns out okay. Or at least they make it look like it turns out okay. And I bet you can name a few former tabloid darlings who are no longer with us — either due to fading away into "Where Are They Now?" status, or, even worse, because they didn't make it through the scandal alive. Unless you happen to employ a personal staff of hundreds to clean up your messes, you might want to think twice before you do anything you wouldn't want your grandmother to see.

On the other hand, it might be good for you to think of yourself as somewhat of a celebrity. Not only because yes, you are fabulous, but also because you never know when the local paparazzi (otherwise known as your classmates) are going to catch you doing something you're not entirely proud of. So whenever you're hanging out with your friends, stop for a minute. Think about whether you would like to see what you're

INTRODUCTION

doing posted on someone's website or making the rounds as a story forwarded to the whole school.

This book will help you sort out the different influences that peer pressure is having on you, in ways that you may not even be aware of. We'll tell you how peer pressure can manipulate you into making some very bad, life-altering decisions about drugs, sex, cheating, stealing, and being cruel to others. You'll see how to find the strength that already exists within you. You'll also learn how to be yourself, no matter what crowd of people you find yourself in. We'll help you see how important it is to be proud of who you are and to surround yourself with real friends who are proud of you, too.

Lisa Medoff, Ph.D.

HOW TO USE THIS BOOK

Chill (Relax)

Absorb more information and practical advice.

FOOD FOR THOUGHT

A study conducted by the University of Michigan found that 1/3 of teens feel stressed out on a daily basis. The leading cause? The feeling of not being able to meet high expectations. Prolonged feelings of stress can lead to frustration, illness, aggression, and depression.

Freaking out. Flipping out. Spazzing. Call it what you want, but one thing's for sure: it's not a good thing to do during a test, although it certainly is easy to do!

Maybe you studied more than you've ever studied before and are psyching yourself out that it'll all be for nothing. Maybe you're encountering tougher questions than you expected. Maybe you're wondering if you maybe studied the wrong chapter!

In any case, it won't do you any good to go ballistic. When you're stressing out, you're not thinking clearly and you're more likely to second

Read these inspirational, witty, or tongue-in-cheek observations that you can use to motivate yourself—or just for fun.

"A problem is a chance for you to do your best."
—Duke Ellington

HOW TO USE THIS BOOK

We created the SOS series to help you find answers to questions most pressing on your mind. In developing this series, we brought together both adult and teen experts who shared their successes and struggles. Here's how to best use this book:

guess your answers and waste more time mulling them over than if you're confident and calm. So if you find yourself sweating under the collar, take a second to breathe deeply, focus, and chill out. It's the best thing you can do for yourself during a test.

F.Y.I.

A few simple ways to manage stress:

1. Positive "Self-Talk" : Try repeating to yourself silently "I can handle this" or "It's going to be O.K." Having a positive attitude can make stress dissapear.

2. See the funny side of life! Look at your situation from a comical perspective and you'll be able to relax, and when you're relaxed you can think more clearly.

DR. LISA SAYS...

When you get the test, take a minute to empty out everything that is cluttering up your brain before you look at any of the questions. Write down all of your mnemonics, formulas, or information that you're afraid that you'll forget or get confused about. This will not only serve as practical help, but it will also calm you down by focusing you on the information, not on the difficulty of the test. You'll see how much you really do know, and you'll be able to tackle the questions with confidence.

> Get expert advice and anecdotes from our series editor, Lisa Medoff, Ph.D.

> Absorb more information and practical advice.

HOW TO USE THIS BOOK

Think kids are the only ones who need to learn something? Advice, inside info, and motivation for the know-it-alls in every kid's life.

Look here for basic info and terminology

---

118 FIGHTING OFF WHAT'S FIGHTING YOU: STRESS M

CHAPTER 12

Fighting Off Wha

What Is It and How Can I

'm so stressed," is son
heard your friends say
Recently, you even find
them when they compla
of homework they have
commitments. But what

PARENT SPEAK

Let's face it, adults know stress. But do you understand how much stress your student is under? A recent poll of high school students revealed that a whopping 70% said that they feel stressed "most of the time." What stress management tools can you share with your kid? Are there experiences you can relate that will help them put things in perspective?

THE BASICS

stress

n. a specific response b
lus, as fear or pain, that
with the normal physiolc
organism.

physical, mental, or emo
"Worry over his job and
under a great stress."

a situation, occurrence,
"The stress of being tra
gave him a pounding he

HOW TO USE THIS BOOK

CHAPTER 12

ighting You: Stress Management

d of It?

've probably
a daily basis.
ming in with
e mounds
after school
ally??

Stress is the way your body reacts to demands placed on it, whether that's your upcoming advanced Algebra exam or dealing with a difficult friend. When you feel stressed by something, your body releases chemicals into your bloodstream. These chemicals can have both positive and negative effects. Sometimes stress makes you work harder to get something done, but stress can also slow you down, especially if you have no way to deal with the extra energy the chemicals produce in you.

o a stimu-
interferes
rium of an

Here, we'll help you understand the causes of stress, signs of stress, how stress affects you, and the best ways to deal with it, because when you've already got so much to do, stress is the last thing you need to worry about.

or tension:
ealth put him

using this:
elevator

FOOD FOR THOUGHT

Many studies suggest that as students get to college, their sleeping schedule suffers greatly. Lack of sleep often results in the inability to concentrate, the need for more naps, and constant fatigue. Try getting a good rest and maybe this will give you more strength to deal with school and other issues.

For fast-acting relief, try slowing down. "

—Lily Tomlin

STRESSED OUT
STUDENTS
GUIDE TO
HANDLING
PEER PRESSURE

Under Pressure

> "Listen to your gut. If you feel uncomfortable, even if your friends seem to be OK with what's going on, it means that something about the situation is wrong for you. This kind of decision-making is part of becoming self-reliant and learning more about who you are."

Pressure, pushing down on me,

Pressing down on you..."

Rockers David Bowie and Freddy Mercury really had it right when they sang that famous song. But c'mon! By then, they were millionaire super-stars and music legends. We only wish we had their kind of pressure. If only the greatest things weighing on us was the decision about what to spend our millions on!

No, the pressures we're more likely to encounter don't come from adoring crowds of admirers, or our tour managers, but instead, from our friends at school. Homework, cheating, drugs and

THE BASICS

peer pressure
n. social pressure by members of one's peer group to take a certain action, adopt certain values, or otherwise conform in order to be accepted.

Definition from dictionary.com

alcohol, cliques, popularity contests, sex... now that's the kind of pressure we're facing here.

Under pressure? Of course you are.

Caving in to it? You don't have to.

FOOD FOR THOUGHT

Are you your toughest critic? Most people who fall to peer pressure admit to being extremely hard on themselves. Sometimes it's easier to pass that critical voice to someone else, but in doing so you give up your power.

DR. LISA SAYS...

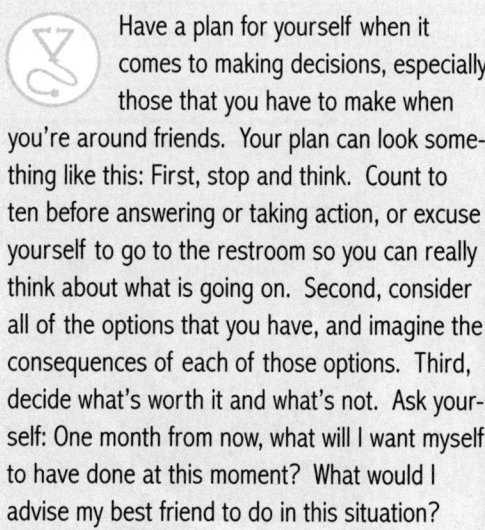

Have a plan for yourself when it comes to making decisions, especially those that you have to make when you're around friends. Your plan can look something like this: First, stop and think. Count to ten before answering or taking action, or excuse yourself to go to the restroom so you can really think about what is going on. Second, consider all of the options that you have, and imagine the consequences of each of those options. Third, decide what's worth it and what's not. Ask yourself: One month from now, what will I want myself to have done at this moment? What would I advise my best friend to do in this situation?

Let's Face It (What It Is)

FOOD FOR THOUGHT

Peer pressure doesn't let up as you get older. Teens face it, college students face it, and adults face it. You'll encounter it at school, at parties, and eventually in the work place. Might as well learn the healthy ways to handle it now!

The fact of the matter is, if you spend a good part of your day with your peers worrying about how they'll see you, trying to fit in with them, and trying to make them happy, you'll feel the pressure several times a day. Peer pressure is the pressure to conform, to act against your will or judgment for social reasons. Peer pressure forces you to do things you are not always comfortable with.

Our technological age has only made peer pressure worse. A nasty rumor or an embarrassing picture can get around to the entire class in one

"He who joyfully marches to music in rank and file has already earned my contempt. He has been given a large brain by mistake, since for him the spinal cord would fully suffice."

—Albert Einstein

night through the power of email or instant messenger. And you may have to resist the urge to sneak a peek at your cell phone when you're taking a test and one of your good friends has texted you the answer to an especially tough question. With so many lines of communication open to today's youth, it's easier and truer than ever to say "everybody's doing it."

But why would you want to be like everybody else?

The truth: if you worry too much about what others think, you risk losing yourself to all their wants and needs. In the worse cases, you could lose your self respect and the ability to make decisions for yourself. Letting other people live your life? Lame.

DR. LISA SAYS...

Think about the people that you really admire, either people that you know or famous people. What do you admire about them? Usually the people that we really look up to are unique in some way. They do their own thing, they stand up for others, and they set the trends instead of following them. Look at famous artists, writers, and musicians — they see the world in a different way than everyone else, and they are able to persuade the rest of us to consider their point of view. Another thing that most famous people have in common is that they have all been criticized by others at some point, but they kept going because they believed in what they were doing.

Peer Pressure (Have You Felt It?)

FOOD FOR THOUGHT

Peer pressure can be both spoken and unspoken. Sometimes the most insidious forms of peer pressure come with no words attached at all—but loads of meaning

Peer pressure. Have you felt it? You have if…

✎ You ever felt like you had to act the way your friends did. You may have thought to yourself, even then, "This isn't me."

✎ You've had an opinion that was unpopular, and people told you to either change it, or shut up.

✎ You've ever been pushed into dating or getting physical with someone you weren't attracted to or interested in.

✎ You were given a cigarette, a joint, or some alcohol, and felt you had to try it so that everyone could see that you were cool, or at least, not uncool.

✎ You heard a nasty rumor about someone, or knew an embarrassing secret, and your friends told you to spill it.

✎ Your friend didn't do his or her homework, or didn't study for a test, and asked to copy from yours. You let them, even though you had spent hours on it.

✎ Your friends decided to ignore one of the girls in your group, even though you're really close. You spent the day pretending you don't like her, because you don't want to be the next one they freeze out.

✎ Your friend has this great new iPod, which he says he pocketed at the store. He wants to get one for you, too, this weekend, even though you insisted you don't want one.

Peer pressure comes at you in many forms, from many directions, and can affect you on a daily basis. Think: what pressure did you face today?

WHAT DO YOU DO?

Your grandmother gave you a new sweater and you love it. Sure it's a little quirky, but it has your favorite colors in it. All 27 of them.

You get to school and your friends wrinkle their nose. "Ug! It's hideous! Take that thing off before we have to burn it!"

> The individual has always had to struggle to keep from being overwhelmed by the tribe. If you try it, you will be lonely often, and sometimes frightened. But no price is too high to pay for the privilege of owning yourself.
>
> —Friedrich Nietzsche

Clique Here — Inner Circles

> Kids ... can get to the point where they feel peer pressure that isn't even there simply because of how they see themselves.

—Walt Mueller, Understanding Today's Youth Culture

"If you're not in, you're out." Silly statement right? Unfortunately, in junior high and high school, it can sometimes seem like being in the "in-crowd" is what it's all about.

Usually several different "crowds" are vying for top spot, each thinking that their way of doing

DR. LISA SAYS...

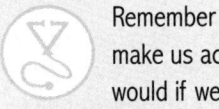

Remember that being in a group can make us act in a way that we never would if we were hanging out one-on-one. Sometimes this can be a good thing — the protection of the group can push us to be more outgoing if we're a bit shy, or to let loose and be silly if we're feeling a bit uptight. Just keep in mind that being in a group of friends might seem to give us permission to be rude or mean to others in order to get attention. Whenever you're with your friends, ask yourself, would I act this way if I were by myself? If not, why? If the answer to that question is because you think the behavior is wrong, then find a way to stop it, or at least excuse yourself from the group for a while.

and Outsiders

things is cooler than the way others do their thing. You know the deal; you're probably in a clique yourself!

Cliques come in all shapes and sizes and members usually gather together because of shared interests or goals. Think of the different cliques at your school. What do you like about them? What don't you like?

Often, cliques get labeled by the actions—or inactions—of its members. If you're part of a clique, there are probably assumptions made about you that may or may not be true. You probably think the same about people in other groups.

There's nothing wrong with having a group of friends. It certainly makes throwing parties, hanging out, and picking lab partners a lot easier. But you're entering a major danger zone if your clique is determining the way you act and completely destroying your own identity.

You know the expression.

"If all of your friends jumped off a bridge. . ."

FOOD FOR THOUGHT

Is there such a thing as positive peer pressure? Of course there is, and we're sure you can think of some examples. The key to dealing is knowing when the pressure you're facing is the good or bad kind.

The Popularity Contest (Why Being Popula

FOOD FOR THOUGHT

Maybe it seems like a good idea to dump your elementary school friend who just isn't into the same things you are now. Or maybe not. Perhaps you really have grown apart, or maybe just your current interests. See if you can find some common ground. It's always easier to keep a good friend than make one.

Sure, being popular comes with a few perks. People want to hang out with you. People want to dress like you. People want to be you. In the microcosm that is junior high or high school, it's easy to see how highly popularity is prized.

Sometimes you can become popular for the way you look or dress, other times it's for achievements and accomplishments. People become unpopular for the same reasons and that's a lot more painful. It's easy to gain perspective when it's happening to someone else, but when you're neck-deep in the politics of school, life can be brutal.

Maybe you can remember some things you've done in hopes of becoming more popular. Bought that new skirt or new pair of sneakers to so you could dress to impress, even though the price tag made you cringe upon first glance? Ditched an unpopular friend so you wouldn't have to hang out with a loser? (What? Were you afraid their uncoolness would somehow rub off on you?)

sn't All That)

We're probably all guilty of a little of this behavior, but the next time you do something for the sake of popularity, remember: it's just school.

Until graduation, it seems like popularity matters more than almost anything else. We promise that even though four years seems like forever, it won't last that long.

WHAT DO YOU DO?

There's a new girl in school and she seems nice.

Then the news breaks: she was kicked out of her old school for having a relationship with her history teacher, who was old enough to be her father. Ew. Now everyone's more interested in talking about her than talking to her.

Should you avoid her like the plague like everyone else is doing?

"I'll never admit it again, but I'd do anything to be popular. If you're not popular, you're pretty much invisible."

Jocks, Emos, Geeks, and Nerds (Cliques

Junior high and high school are environments where, for some reason, teens feel the urge to travel in packs. Based on shared interests and personalities, what usually happens is the formation of cliques that you can find variations at practically every school campus across the country: jocks, cheerleaders, nerds, band geeks, emo kids, drama freaks, and so on.

Sometimes it feels like cliques all have their own sets of unspoken rules. Atheletes don't care about academics, nerds shouldn't play sports, If you're a cheerleader, everything in your ward-

FOOD FOR THOUGHT

Students who are called "loners" experience the same issues of fear, acceptance and identity confusion that all teens experience—and are generally well adjusted, just introverted. It takes the same skills to make one or two friends as it does a handful, so don't judge someone's value by the number of kids in their group.

"High school is all about cliques. The only reason I am who I am today is because I was rejected by the athletes, the mathletes, the rich kids, the potheads, the Jewish kids and the glee club. I was left with only the Dungeons and Dragons Society, the student government and the audio / visual club. You put those together, you get my show."

—Stephen Colbert, The Colbert Report

nd Why It's Okay if You Aren't In One)

robe has to be cute, sexy, or both.

If you identify with a clique at your school, that's perfectly fine. But if you're not in a clique and are what your peers may call a "loner," don't sweat it. You wear what you want to wear. You carve your own path, and live by your own rules. If you're happy with yourself without the validation of a group of your peers, guess what? You're saving yourself a whole lot of emotional struggle. More power to ya.

THE F.Y.I.

Famous (and cool!) loner- type personalities:
James Dean
Albert Einstein
Emily Dickenson
J.D. Salinger
Charles Schulz
Virginia Woolf
Charlotte Bronte
Barry Bonds
Orville Wright

" I'm not really in a clique, but I do have friends at school. I have lots of different interests and people I hang out with in these different classes and activities. I think I'm pretty lucky to have good friends and not have to deal with all that drama. "

Inside Looking Out (Accepting People Wh

"This guy started school last week, mid-semester, and he seemed really weird. Everybody was making fun of his shoes and awkwardness. Then it turned out that he was someone I'd gone to elementary school with and played with growing up. It felt bad when I realized that I hadn't given him a chance."

If the life of a loner simply isn't for you, then you're probably on the inside (of a clique, that is) looking out. You may have noticed that when people get together, they can be harsh in the way they judge outsiders. It's a sad fact of human nature: we fear what we don't understand.

But you can live above all that. The next time you see someone wearing something you and your clique don't approve of, stop yourself and say... "Hey! It's probably cool somewhere in the world!" or consider that person's wardrobe choice ahead of its time.

The next time you see someone stand up for something unpopular or controversial, think twice before you join the mob in tearing that per-

No person is your friend who demands your silence, or denies your right to grow.

——Alice Walker

.ren't Like You)

son down Remember, "It's a free country." We're all free to do and think as we want. Kudos to that person for exercising his or her rights!

FOOD FOR THOUGHT

We all love and admire them now, but some of your favorite celebrities used to be outsiders. Next time your friends make fun of someone for their style, you should wonder if that person will end up more glamorous than all of you combined.

Natalie Portman was a straight-A student in high school.

Vin Diesel has been a hardcore 'Dungeons and Dragons' fan for over 20 years.

Josh Hartnett is a huge Star Wars fan and admits to having spent much of his time reading alone.

Cher admits to being very lonely and introverted early in her career.

Tom Hanks had to move from school to school because of his father's job, and as a result was painfully shy in his childhood.

Gene Simmons – hardcore rocker of the band KISS - has said that he prefers his privacy.

R–E–S–P–E–C–T (Treating People Righ

The fact of the matter is that no one likes being pressured to be something they're not, or to do something that's not natural to them. As often as you feel pressured by others, consider for a second the ways in which you may be giving as good as you're getting.

Stepping back and letting someone make a decision on their own, based on their values and needs, is showing respect for that person's autonomy or independence. And strongarming someone is very definitely a sign of "dis"respect.

If you're asking someone to change just because you're personally uncomfortable with something

FOOD FOR THOUGHT

It's much easier to show respect for others when you have been respected. Keep this in mind when you are interacting with your peers. Show some respect and maybe they'll pass it on

"When we show our respect for other living things, they respond with respect for us."

—Arapaho Proverb

ven When Others Don't)

that's basic to their character or style, or if you're pressing someone to do something with you just because you'd like someone to have your back and be your partner in crime, stop for a second and think about it. Are you using your powers of persuasion or friendship for evil? In other words, check yourself before you wreck yourself and someone else along with you. That's respect, my friend.

DR. LISA SAYS...

Are there people at your school that seem to be friends with everyone? They don't seem to fit into one group, but yet they fit in everywhere. Watch these people carefully, and learn from them. How do they carry themselves? How do they treat others? Do they seem to spend a lot of time worried about what others will think? Usually these people are confident, have a good sense of humor, don't take themselves too seriously, and are kind to everyone.

"Kids are always talking about being disrespected, and it's cool to be rude to someone else. Why can't it be cool to respect your friends and class-mates?"

Stuff You Don't Want To Talk

"When I lost my virgin-ity, I did it 'cause I thought he'd beome my boy-friend if I did. He didn't."

Birds do it, bees do it, but you'll never see one blue jay chirping to another, "Hey, bro. Did you score with that chick last night?"

DR. LISA SAYS...

The best thing for you to do is when it comes to sex is to get as much information as you can from lots of different sources, and then make a decision that feels comfortable for you. If you want to make a different decision tomorrow, then that's okay, too. Talk over your feelings and choices with a friend or adult that you trust — someone that you know has your best interests in mind. It can also be helpful to find websites that have cred-ible information about sex and health, such as those that are put out by hospitals or adoles-cent health centers. You can ask your doctor, health teacher, or reference librarian for some good places to start. Don't be embarrassed — you're not going to be the only person asking.

To Your Parents About (Sex)

When it comes to sex, we humans, and especially teen humans' face a lot of pressure. More than just deciding if you're ready for sex, you're probably also concerned and confused about STDs, pregnancy risk, technique, and how your reputation will change after you do it.

Your confusion about sex is well placed; in some ways sex remains confusing and complicated well into adulthood. Bottom line: if you're not ready to do it, do not give in to pressure to do it, even if the pressure comes from your boyfriend or girlfriend and you're "official." The emotional risks are real, the health risks are real, and the regrets can be really real.

FOOD FOR THOUGHT

While there's lot of pressure for both guys and girls to be sexually active, recent research shows that most high school kids are not having sex. So don't think you have to hook up to be liked. 'Cause you don't.

The people in the popular group say there is no peer pressure because they are at the top of the food chain. Really what they are doing is just eating away at everybody else.

—Lauren Greenfield, Girl Culture

Everybody's Doing It (Misconceptions Abou

"C'mon! Everybody's doing it!"

Newsflash: No they aren't. And remember that looks can be deceiving. With so many people projecting an image of sex and sexiness all the time—from your classmates to the rap artists and pop princesses you see on MTV—it's easy to see why you might be under the impression that casual sex is rampant. That's simply not the case. The truth is, it gets talked about far more often than it actually gets done.

Some boyfriends and girlfriends might have you believe that when you're in a relationship, it's

FOOD FOR THOUGHT

Nationally, more than 50% of teens remain virgins until they are at least 17 years of age. If most of your friends claim to have had sex… chances are at least some of them are straight up liars.

> From the belly rings and the tight tank tops to the music lyrics they recite in the hallways, school is a sexually charged environment.
>
> —Mr. Maxson, 8th grade science

ex)

your duty to put out. That's possibly the most damaging misconception of all. Being in a relationship requires only that you care about and support your significant other. If it's true and meant to be, he or she will wait until you're ready to take that step – not a minute before.

And if they won't, they don't respect you. It's a harsh reality, but the truth. You should, and will, find someone who does respect you. Really.

> "Not everybody's doing it. But everybody's lying about it."

F.Y.I.

You get some really mixed up messages about sex. Your parents and teachers may be telling you never to do it, your friends are telling you that you should be doing it, and movies & television seem to be telling you that it's the only important thing in the world. How are you supposed to figure out what you want? That's the most important question – what do you want? And whatever it is that you want, who do you want to share it with? No one else, no one, can tell you what you should do with your body. Spend some time thinking about what you want before you head out on a date or to a party. Practice putting what you want into words, and don't let anyone talk you into doing anything different. Always have an escape plan in case things start to feel out of control.

Kiss and Tell (When Everyone Else is Talkir

PARENT SPEAK

As a parent, it's hard enough to think your son or daughter will ever be sexually active. But it's absolutely heart wrenching to hear that your child's private life is the fodder for gossips. Get the real story from your student, and don't assume anything.

M any girls you know may like to show off their bodies with revealing clothing, and you definitely can name some guys who can't be stopped when it comes to flirting. Reminders of our hormonal urges are everywhere... and people like talking about sex just as much as they like thinking about it.

Gossip mongers like dirty details. They feed on them, and after a hot date, you can be sure they'll be interested. You have a decision to make, and a difficult one when the person asking the questions is a friend. You may be tempted to give up the info, or to suggest something that didn't really happen just to satisfy them, but just remember that they're only satisfied when they've taken that bit of information and passed

"Never kiss and tell."

—Unknown

\bout It)

it along to someone else. Before you know it, everyone knows your business, and you've hurt someone you probably care a lot about.

When the pressure's on to kiss and tell, the best move is probably just to tell curious people to back off!

If something did happen, you can still maintain a "cool" image without hurting anyone by refusing to give out any details. Mystery can be intriguing...

THE F.Y.I.

Keeping it Real, Keeping your Cool

If someone's bugging you to give up the hot details of your date, you can always say: "We played Scrabble for three hours and she came up with the word 'callipygian' (It means 'possessing shapely buttocks'). How's that for a hot detail?"

" I told my friends that I hooked up with this girl at school. All of a sudden, I'm this cool guy and she's a slut—and nothing ever happened. "

No Means No Means NO! (Knowing Wher

FOOD FOR THOUGHT

According to the U.S. Justice Department, one in two rape victims is under age 18.

"Since we all came from a woman, got our name from a woman, and our game from a woman. I wonder why we take from women, why we rape our women, do we hate our women? I think its time we killed for our women, be real to our women, try to heal our women, cus if we dont we'll have a race of babies that will hate the ladies, who make the babies. And since a man can't make one he has no right to tell a women when and where to create one."

—Tupac Shakur

You're Not Ready)

The night's been going great, you're feeling the attraction, and one of you is feeling the animal urges.

If that person is, unfortunately, not you, then you're facing quite the awkward situation. You may really want the other person to like you, or you may just want to save that person some embarrassment. Either way, if you're not ready, it's never a good idea to give in to pressure and give it up. It doesn't matter if you've gone much farther with someone else in the past or if it's your fifth or fiftieth date with the same person. If you don't want to have sex, you have to let him or her know.

You hear it all the time. "No means no." Not "unless the guy/girl spent a lot of money on me," and/or "but yes if he/she threatens to break up with me." NO MEANS NO. Period.

And if you're forced to have sex against your wishes, first understand that IT IS NOT YOUR FAULT. Second, report it. If you can't go to your parents, tell a trusted adult, such as a teacher, counselor, or family friend.

THE F.Y.I.

Nationally, 6 out of 10 girls who had sex before the age of 15 report that it was involuntary. That's assault.

Alcohol and Alcohol Abuse

> "It's what we do when we get together on the weekends. What else do kids do?"

Ads for alcohol are everywhere, and they almost always present drinks as fun, sexy and sophisticated. Still, maybe you're 16 and not interested in breaking the law. When you really think about it, you can certainly afford to keep sipping on that Gatorade or Sunny D for a few more years. No sweat.

Your judgment may get a little fuzzy, however, when you're at a party or with a group of friends and someone hands you a bottle. "What's the harm in taking a little swig when there are no cops around?" you might think.

THE BASICS

alcoholism

n. a chronic disorder characterized by dependence on alcohol, repeated excessive use of alcoholic beverages, the development of withdrawal symptoms on reducing or ceasing intake, morbidity that may include cirrhosis of the liver, and decreased ability to function socially and vocationally.

Definition from dictionary.com

Things can quickly escalate out of control. Being young and having little to no built up tolerance for alcohol means you can go overboard fast. Trying to make it home for curfew, you may end up with a DUI, or worse. Without a controlled, adult social context for the drinking, you may hit that bottle too hard and start yourself on the path towards alcoholism. There is nothing fun, sexy or sophisticated about rehab.

Believe it or not, we've actually sent students home from school for being drunk and/or high. In all my years of teaching, I never imagined I would see this.

—Ms. Higgenbotham, 11th grade Spanish

FOOD FOR THOUGHT

28.2 percent of 12- to 20-year-olds reported drinking alcohol in the previous month. 18.8 percent of underage drinkers were binge drinkers and 6 percent were heavy drinkers. To compare, if you just look at the number of high school kids who drank in that month, the percentage increases to 43.3

Source: U.S. Department of Health and Human Services

Getting the Buzz (Everyone's Talking Abou

"**M**an, I was totally wasted last night."

"Guys, I'm feeling buzzed."

"Let's get drunk!"

You probably hear these phrases get tossed around fairly often. People who say them know that they're making themselves out to be rebels or hard partyers.

But just like with sex, not everyone who talks about it is actually doing it. Alcohol is expensive.

THE BASICS

wasted

adj. waste.

done to no avail;

useless: wasted

efforts.

physically or

psychologically

exhausted;

debilitated: to be

wasted by a long

illness.

" I don't really drink, but I talk a lot about drinking. It makes me seem cooler than I really am. "

t, Not Everyone's Doing It)

It makes it very hard to do work – homework or otherwise, and the consequences of getting caught with it before you're 21 are not pretty. Most of your classmates are probably smart enough to know that getting drunk frequently is no way for a student to get ahead in life.

So the next time someone brags to you about getting drunk, don't take it as a cue to start drinking more so you can talk about it. Realize that you just might be talking to someone who wants your attention.

PARENT SPEAK

Some parents consider a "little" drinking in high school totally harmless. Did you know it also :

✓ negatively affects your child's brain funtion

✓ slows the learning process, resulting in poor grades

✓ contributes to depression and suicidal thoughts

✓ exacerbates a tendency toward violence

✓ encourages truancy

✓ risks dependency at a younger age

Fake IDs and DUIs (Reasons Not To Drink)

FOOD FOR THOUGHT

Most states will take away your driver's license until you are 18 if you are caught drinking and driving (plus other fines and penalties). And that's the least of your worries. You could get into an accident and hurt someone else, or yourself.

The problem with being a teenager is that you always want what's just a few years down the line. First it's driving, and then it's graduation, but once you're finally behind the wheel and your diploma is on the wall, the next big milestone is being old enough to drink.

You probably know plenty of people who just couldn't wait those extra years however, and have gone completely out of their way to be able to cheat the system. Case in point: fake IDs. A good, authentic-looking fake ID can cost up to a few hundred dollars.

But if you think the worst thing that can happen if you're caught drinking underage or with a fake

PARENT SPEAK

A fake ID is something most of us have had. But today's stakes are a bit different. In some states, using a fake driver's license can land you a felony conviction. A felony is very serious and, in the long term will affect your son or daughter more seriously than a bad grade or poor test scores.

ID is that you'll be kicked out of the bar, guess again. Getting caught can mean a conviction of a Class 3 misdemeanor, a fine, community service, and a suspension of your driver license of up to one year. And if we're talking about a DUI, it gets much, much worse. Your license can be revoked, you can be on probation, and you can even face jail time.

You don't even have to use your fake I.D. to face legal consequences. The police officer won't care when you tell him, "But I've never even used it."

THE F.Y.I.

Keeping it Real, Keeping your Cool

If someone keeps pestering you to drink despite your telling them repeatedly that you don't want to, you can always say: "No, the last time I was swigging alcohol, the paparazzi snapped some pictures that ended up all over the pages of People Magazine. If I drink again, my publicist will kill me. What? You didn't know I was a huge pop star?"

" I ordered a fake ID online, from the comfort of my bedroom. It arrived within a week and my parents never knew. "

Boo to Booze (Turning Down the Bottle)

FOOD FOR THOUGHT

Adults age 21 and older who had their first drink before they were of legal drinking age were significantly more likely to become dependent on alcohol or to abuse it.

2005 SAMHSA National Survey on Drug Use and Health

Everything stacked up, drinking before you're of legal age is just not worth it. Even if you realize it, many of your peers may not, and then the problem of peer pressure still exists.

If you're offered alcohol and you're just not feeling it, there are plenty of tactful ways of turning down the bottle without being a buzzkill, so to speak. Try these:

"No thanks. I like to keep a clear head."

"My parents will kill me. Seriously. Or they'll punish me so badly I'd wish I were dead."

"Underage drinking costs the United States more than $62 billion each year. At this crucial time when research shows that girls are binge drinking with alarming regularity, more must be done to reduce youth access to alcohol, and the appeal of alcohol to our youth."

—David Jernigan

"Naw. I stay away from that stuff."

Or why not just say it straight? Sometimes there's beauty in simplicity:
"No thanks. I don't drink."

PARENT SPEAK

These 7 steps should help you be as prepared as possible to help deter your children from underage drinking.

✓ Set a good example for your children regarding the use of alcohol.
✓ Encourage your children to talk with you about their problems and concerns.
✓ Get to know your children's friends and discuss ways your children can avoid drinking when they are feeling pressured by peers.
✓ Talk to other parents about ways to send a consistent, clear message that underage drinking is not acceptable behavior or a "rite of passage."
✓ Encourage your children to participate in supervised activities and events that are challenging, fun and alcohol free.
✓ Learn the warning signs that indicate your children may be drinking and act promptly to get help.
✓ Make sure you're at home for all your children's parties and be sure those parties are alcohol free.

www.parentingisprevention.org

CHAPTER 5

The Hard Stuff—Cancer Sticks,

> "Drugs are a waste of time. They destroy your memory and your self-re-spect and ev-erything that goes along with your self esteem."
>
> —Kurt Cobain

Let's cut to the chase on this one. It's more than just the inconvenience of community service, more than disappointing your parents, or a blemish on your permanent record. Doing drugs can ruin your life.

This probably sounds as crazy and reactionary to you, as it has to generations before you. But it's

PARENT SPEAK

If you think your child, or one of their peers is using drugs, you'll probably be tipped off by something that seems a little off. The following are things that may indicate drug use. The student may:

✓ have trouble concentrating
✓ seem disinterested in school or friends
✓ suddenly makes a whole new set of friends
✓ sleep a lot
✓ act moody or negative
✓ get in fights or arguments
✓ have puffy or red eyes
✓ have a persistent cough or runny nose

Drugs and Illegal Substances

the truth, and a truth you should take to heart. Drug use can undermine your academic career and alienate you from friends and family. It's an extracurricular activity no one wants or needs on their resume.

You'll probably first encounter the "opportunity" to do drugs in a party-type situation. It might be a small private gathering in someone's basement, or a loud, crowded club. Wherever it happens, what you decide to do then can determine your life's path for years and years there-after.

Are you ready to give up on your dreams? Are you ready to spend lots of money to feed an addiction? Are you ready to risk your life? Are you ready to lose everything you love?

Let's take a closer look.

DR. LISA SAYS...

It's a lot easier to resist peer pressure in the moment if you're really clear ahead of time about your own feelings about drugs and alcohol. Are you an athlete who needs to stay away from unhealthy substances in order to make sure your performance stays at an optimal level? Have you invested too much time and effort in your brain to take a risk destroying it with one night of craziness? Are you unwilling to give up control of your body and behavior? Spend some time answering these questions for yourself before you head out for the night, and be prepared to explain those answers to your friends.

It's In The Air (Tobacco and Marijuana)

FOOD FOR THOUGHT

Marijuana goes by many names:
Pot
Weed
Ganja
Boom
Chronic
Grass
Herb
Reefer
Dope

No matter the name it goes by, what it spells is t-r-o-u-b-l-e.

You know by now the risks associated with smoking. If you haven't learned about them through anti-drug programs at school or public service announcements on TV, they're printed right on the cigarette box: emphysema, birth defects, heart disease, lung cancer...

If, somehow, those don't deter you from lighting up the first time someone hands you a cigarette, consider the money you'll waste on buying those cancer sticks for years and years, how bad your breath, hair, and furniture will smell. Consider all this together, and the answer is clear when you're facing peer pressure to smoke.

"It is easy to get a thousand prescriptions but hard to get one single remedy."

—Chinese Proverb

Similarly easy to get, and easily as addictive is marijuana. Of all the illegal substances you might be offered, this is the one you will most likely encounter first. The addiction to weed, unlike cigarettes, isn't caused by nicotine; it's caused by an artificial euphoric high, and the strong desire to experience it again. If you welcome the idea of being a slave to an addiction that makes it nearly impossible to study, work, or even concentrate on your hobbies, you might as well give it a try. If you don't mind going to jail for something stupid like possession or destroying your chances of getting in a good college or landing that dream job, go ahead; take a hit.

But if you're smart enough to see why it simply isn't worth the risk, then peer pressure in this area is no problem for you.

FOOD FOR THOUGHT

Marijuana is the most commonly used illicit drug; some 77 percent of current illicit drug users use marijuana. According to the National Household Survey on Drug Abuse, in 1995 an estimated 12.8 million Americans were current illicit drug users -- meaning they had used an illicit drug in the month prior to the survey. This represents 6.1 percent of the population 12 years old and older.

Source: National Household Survey on Drug Abuse

Over the Counter (Pharmaceuticals)

FOOD FOR THOUGHT

Prescription medication abuse by teens and young adults is a serious problem in the United States.

✓ 1 in 5 teens has abused a prescription pain medication

✓ 1 in 5 report abusing prescription stimulants and tranquilizers

✓ 1 in 10 has abused cough medication

Source: Partnership for a Drug Free America

Y ou go over to your friend's house and, with a mischievous look he or she hands you a little pill.

"My mom takes these for her pain. Go ahead, pop one."

You hesitate, but you consider it. The first thought that occurs to you as you look at the eager expression on your friends' face is, "Well… it has to be safe right? It was prescribed by a doctor."

Wrong. Even if a drug was formulated to cure an ailment, manage pain, or control the symptoms of a disease, the fact of the matter is any uninformed use of a strong substance can have serious health risks. You can probably think of certain celebrities who have accidentally taken the wrong combination of pills, and ended up as fallen stars. Even something that is typically harmless like cough medicine, can wreak havoc on your body if abused.

Give the pill back and tell your friend you love your life too much to dull it away or risk it for a high.

PARENT SPEAK

Prescription drug abuse is an increasingly disturbing problem for middle school and high school students. An estimated 20 percent of people in the United States have used prescription drugs for nonmedical reasons. This is prescription drug abuse. It is a serious and growing problem.

Abusing some prescription drugs can lead to addiction. You can develop an addiction to:

✓ Narcotic painkillers
✓ Sedatives and tranquilizers
✓ Stimulants

Experts don't know exactly why this type of drug abuse is increasing. The availability of drugs is probably one reason. Doctors are prescribing more drugs for more health problems than ever before. Online pharmacies make it easy to get prescription drugs without a prescription, even for kids.

Source: National Institute on Drug Abuse

"Kids bring their parents' drugs to school all the time: sleeping pills, pain killers, allergy meds—pretty much everything. It's like candy."

Under Your Skin (Hard Drugs)

FOOD FOR THOUGHT

The increase in the use of marijuana has been especially pronounced. Between 1992 and 2005 past-month use of marijuana increased from:

✓ 12% to 20% among high school seniors.
✓ 8% to 15% among 10th graders.
✓ 4% to 7% among 8th graders.

Reported use of marijuana by high school seniors during a month peaked in 1978 at 37% and declined to its lowest level in 1992 at 12%.

The use of cocaine within the past month of the survey by high school seniors peaked in 1985 at 6.7%, up from 1.9% in 1975 at the survey's inception. Cocaine use declined to a low of 1.3% in 1992 and 1993. In 2005, 2.3% of high school seniors reported past-month cocaine use.

Source: University of Michigan, Monitoring the Future National Results on Adolescent Drug Use: Overview of Key Findings 2005, April 2006.

In a recent lab study, it was discovered that rhesus monkeys who were addicted to cocaine, when given the choice, chose the drug over food, even when they were starving. That's right: their need to feed their addiction overrode their instinct to survive.

Hard drugs are injected, snorted, or ingested. People who are addicted feed them directly into their systems and live from high to high. They become drug-seeking machines— slaves to substances. Until they find a way to kick their habits, they have no hopes, dreams, ambitions or better judgment.

Their lives become about the drugs.

What else is there that needs to be said? More so than with anything mentioned in this book, the decision to resist peer pressure in this area should be an easy one.

DR. LISA SAYS...

 Lots of celebrities end up in rehab, and the whole experience may actually sound cool to you. Go crazy partying for a few months, head off for another few months of rest and relaxation, and return looking even more gorgeous than ever. However, your experience will be quite different. Chances are, you don't have the money to go to the kind of posh retreats that celebrities frequent. Rehab for real people is not the beautiful, tranquil place that you see on television — it can actually be quite ugly and scary. Plus, you also probably don't have the millions in your bank account that will allow you to do things like hiring an expensive lawyer to keep you out of jail or picking up your life right where you left off.

"Today's students can put dope in their veins or hope in their brains. If they can conceive it and believe it, they can achieve it. They must know it is not their aptitude but their attitude that will determine their altitude."
—Jesse Jackson

Drug Abuse = Drugs Abusing You (Reason

PARENT SPEAK

The following are key talking points for discussing drug use with your child:

✓ We are here to make it clear that we will not tolerate any drug or alcohol use by you.

✓ We have rules in the family. The rules do not permit teen drug and alcohol use.

✓ Even though you think everyone is using drugs or alcohol, it is illegal and not allowable.

✓ You can endanger your life and the lives of others. We don't want anything bad to happen to you. I don't know what I'd do if I lost you.

✓ We count on you as a family member. Your brothers and sisters look up to you and care about you. What would they do if you were gone?

✓ Drug and alcohol use can ruin your future and chances to…graduate, go to college, get a job, and keep your driver's license.

✓ We are here to support you. What can I do to help you not use?

✓ Sometimes kids use drugs and alcohol because there are other issues going on like stress, unhappiness and social issues. Have you thought about this? Are there other problems you want to talk about?

✓ Are your friends using? How are you handling that? Is it hard to not use in that environment?

✓ We won't give up on you because we love you. We're going to be on your case until you stop completely. If you need professional help, we will be there to support you and help make it happen.

Source: TheAntiDrug.com

ot To Do Them)

Need more convincing to counteract all the peer pressure you're getting to do drugs? Here are some good reasons for you. Feel free to pass them on:

✎ Have you ever pictured yourself living on the streets? Feeding a serious drug addiction can cost you up to several hundred dollars a day. Not even someone on a doctor's salary can afford to be addicted for very long.

✎ Crack, meth, and ecstasy can cause heart attacks or strokes. Sharing needles in a drug-induced haze can easily lead to contracting HIV/AIDS.

✎ Arguably, the worst problems facing society are prostitution, weapons, and drugs. Many prostitutes were forced into the trade by their dealers in order to pay for their drugs. The illegal weapons trade is largely fueled by dealers trying to protect their "business." When you pay to use drugs, you are not only harming yourself, you are literally harming everyone around you. You become part of the problem.

> My parents talked to me about drugs as if I didn't know anything at all. But I knew a lot more than they thought I did.

THE BASICS

ad•dict
n. a person who is addicted to an activity, habit, or substance: a drug addict.
v. cause to become physiologically or psychologically dependent on an addictive substance, as alcohol or a narcotic.

Definition from Dictionary.com

Just Say No, Live Above the Influence (No

FOOD FOR THOUGHT

A recent study by the Met Life Foundation found that when parents talk to kids about alcohol and drug abuse, teens take their parents' messages to heart — only 16 percent of teens whose parents set a zero tolerance policy reported their individual likelihood of using drugs or alcohol, whereas 45 percent of teens whose parents didn't set such boundaries reported they were likely to drink or use drugs at prom or graduation parties.

Considering all the awful things drugs and alcohol can do to your life, and considering all the precious things you can lose to addictions, you really gotta wonder...

Are the people pressuring you to do these things really your friends?

If they are, then they not only need you to refuse the drugs, but they need you to use your clear-headedness to help them kick their own addictions.

"I think it's an honor to be a role model to one person or maybe more than that. If you are given a chance to be a role model, I think you should always take it because you can influence a person's life in a positive light, and that's what I want to do. That's what it's all about."

—Tiger Woods

ıst Clichés)

Confront them. The truth can hurt, but if their addictions are affecting their lives, they need to hear the truth, and it's better coming from you than from a law enforcement officer or a judge in a court of law. Don't be afraid to use your friendship as leverage. This falls in the category of positive peer pressure, and it's one area where applying the pressure and applying it hard, makes you a hero. You may even save their lives.

THE BASICS

role model
n. a person whose behavior, example, or success is or can be emulated by others, esp. by younger people.

*Definition from
Dictionary.com*

PARENT SPEAK

Be a Good Role Model

Be a role model of the person you want your kid to be. What stronger anti-drug message is there?

Keep these tips in mind:

Be a living, day-to-day example of your value system. Show the compassion, honesty, generosity and openness you want your child to have.

Know that there is no such thing as "do as I say, not as I do" when it comes to drugs. If you take drugs, you can't expect your child to take your advice. Seek professional help if necessary.

Examine your own behavior. If you abuse drugs or alcohol, your kids are going to pick up on it. Or if you laugh at a drunk or stoned person in a movie, you may be sending the wrong message to your child. Be the person you want your kid to be. What stronger anti-drug message is there?

Source: The National Youth Anti-Drug Media Campaign's Behavior Change Expert Panel

Shortcuts: A Long Way To

> "If you're not at the top of the class, there's a feeling that you just shouldn't be there. The teachers don't say it, but you can feel it."

Maybe you studied and studied and studied and you still don't understand the material you're about to be tested on.

Maybe you should have studied, but you were out too late last night, having too much fun.

Maybe you think you're ready for the test, but you're so nervous that you might not do well because of sheer anxiety.

The question has probably, at this point, crossed your mind: "Should I cheat?"

F.Y.I.

It's impossible to find a teacher who would hesitate for even a second to give you a big fat "0" if they caught you cheating. You may even get kicked out of school. After high school when you move along to college or begin working, the consequences for cheating in any form become significantly more dire.

Fall – Cheating

You may wonder, "Who would I be hurting, anyway, if I cheated on this test?"

Choose carefully. Is it:
a) nobody
b) your teacher
c) whatever higher power is watching you
d) yourself

No need to peek at the answers, we'll give it to you: It's d) yourself. Read on.

PARENT SPEAK

Unfortunately, the pressure to excel at school often outweighs common sense or ethics. Everyone wants to succeed and no one wants to be left behind. How can you help your child do well and maintain their integrity?

DR. LISA SAYS...

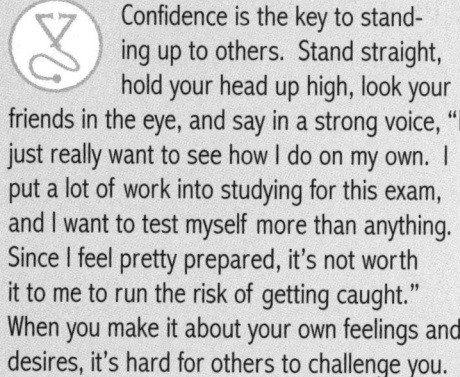

Confidence is the key to standing up to others. Stand straight, hold your head up high, look your friends in the eye, and say in a strong voice, "I just really want to see how I do on my own. I put a lot of work into studying for this exam, and I want to test myself more than anything. Since I feel pretty prepared, it's not worth it to me to run the risk of getting caught." When you make it about your own feelings and desires, it's hard for others to challenge you.

The A–Game (Where the Pressure Come

FOOD FOR THOUGHT

Pressure by parents and schools to achieve top scores has created stress levels among students—beginning as early as elementary school—that are so high that some educators regard it as a health epidemic, said Denise Clark Pope, a lecturer in the School of Education and the author of Doing School: How We Are Creating a Generation of Stressed Out, Materialistic and Miseducated Students. "The number one cause of visits to the health center used to be relationships, but now is stress and anxiety," she said.

You've heard it a million times: You have to get good grades in school. You have to score high on the SAT or ACT. You have to choose activities that demonstrate your leadership qualities. You have to do all these things or else you won't get into a good college, and if you don't go to college, you won't get a good job and you'll be poor and miserable.

"If you don't quit, and don't cheat, and don't run home when trouble arrives, you can only win."

—Shelley Long

rom)

Of course, this is an exaggeration. If you take a cross section of all the successful people in our country and in the world, you'll find an eclectic mix of approaches and lifestyles, some involving college, some not. But when you're in high school and the future is looming, this is little comfort.

It may be your parents pressuring you to get as many A's as you can, or you may be heaping the pressure on yourself. Either way, at times you may feel the urge to do something drastic to get ahead.

THE F.Y.I.

More and more teachers are using an online service called turnitin.com to detect plagiarism in papers, and it is highly effective. Institutions that use it report major drops in plagiarism rates.

"Yes, I cheat. Everyone cheats at my school and the teachers have to know about it. I mean, really, how many A's can a teacher give out before he gets suspicious."

You Don't "Score!" When You Cheat (Wh

FOOD FOR THOUGHT

60.8% of college students surveyed have cheated. Of students who cheat, only 16.5% feel bad about it.

"I really need to ace this test. I'll cheat just this once, and then I'll never do it again."

If only things always worked out the way we planned!

Cheating, like a lot of things we know better than to do, presents a slippery slope. Once you've done it once, it's an option that immediately goes back on the table when you're faced with another hard test or assignment. Your integrity, once gone, is difficult to regain.

"It is impossible for a man to be cheated by anyone but himself."

—Ralph Waldo Emerson

t Doesn't Pay to Cheat)

To make matters more complicated, the people who urge you to cheat may think they are helping you, in a twisted sort of way. You may also find out that other people—peers you like and respect—are cheating, and that might make it seem less wrong.

But it isn't. Ask yourself, "am I ready to be a cheater?" Even if you don't get caught, it's a secret that you will have to live with.

F.Y.I.

If you get caught cheating just once, you can...

✓ Lose your parents' trust.

✓ Have a mark on your school record that will hurt your chances of getting into the college of your choice.

✓ Be branded by your peers as a cheater.

✓ Lose your dignity and respect for yourself.

> I found the test answers in the Trash on our class computer's desktop. It was so easy that I thought it was a trick. I was so scared. But I used the answers anyway.

Making the Grade (Resisting the Urge an

FOOD FOR THOUGHT

Nearly all teens in a national, random-sample survey said cheating's wrong. Most who admitted to cheating say it was a rare thing. And fewer than three in 10 said "most" or "a lot" of kids in their school cheat; 44 percent said it's just "some."

"*S*uccessful" cheaters can always find a way to avoid real work and real effort. To avoid getting caught, they have to be incredibly crafty and creative, or they have to lessen the severity of potential punishment by involving as many people in their cheating schemes as possible. If only they invested that ingenuity into doing things the proper way, imagine all the great things they could accomplish!

The problem with consummate cheaters is, when they are faced with situations in which it's impossible for them to cheat, they find themselves

"I didn't think there was anything wrong with it. We were all sharing answers and it seemed like the only way to get all our projects done."

ˈressure to Cheat)

without the work ethic or skills to succeed. They've essentially cheated themselves out of opportunity and valuable experience.

At the end of the day, isn't it much better to take your poor grade, and keep your integrity?

DR. LISA SAYS...

Pressure from friends and classmates is probably the hardest thing to overcome when you're thinking about cheating. You're torn between loyalty and honor, which are two equally important values. The best way to deal with these situations is to stay out of them in the first place. Find ways to avoid being set up, such as offering to help friends study ahead of time. You may even have to steer clear of that friend who always asks to copy your homework after math class is over.

F.Y.I.

An easy life lesson that will help you immeasurably the sooner you learn it is to "just show up." If you have a test and you haven't prepared as well as you should have, just show up. Just being present is often more than half the battle. Things will only get better if you just show up.

Ring the Alarm – Stealing

> It was really easy to do—I started to forget it was even wrong until my Mom started asking where all the games came from and I couldn't come up with a good answer.

We all wish we had that fancy car Donald Trump is driving, or that gorgeous designer dress Keira Knightly wore to the Oscars. Would most of us go as far as to break into a store or a car dealership to get them? (Let's hope the answer is no)

But it's an entirely different story if it's a cute necklace at the mall, or maybe a video game at the electronics store. When you see something you really, really want, when you don't have the money right then, and when the opportunity

F.Y.I.

What is Shoplifting, Really?

✓ Changing price tags or merchandise labels

✓ Consuming food or drink and not paying for it

✓ Walking out of a store wearing unpaid merchandise

✓ Leaving a store without paying for your items

✓ Leaving a restaurant without paying the bill

and Shoplifting

presents itself, the following thought may cross your mind:

"What if I just stick it in my purse/pocket? Would anyone even notice?"

Do you do it? Now imagine your friend is there whispering in your ear:

"Just take it. I'll tell you when the coast is clear. This is gonna be so awesome."

A Pennsylvania woman convicted for shoplifting was sentenced to wear a badge that reads "Convicted Shoplifter." However, her lawyers hope to plea bargain down to a bumper sticker reading "I'd Rather Be Stealing!"

—Jimmy Fallon

FOOD FOR THOUGHT

Penalties and Punishments for Juvenile Shoplifting Include:

✓ Detention (placement or camp)

✓ Probation

✓ Juvenile record

✓ Fines

✓ Community Service

It's in the Bag (Why There's Pressure to Steal)

PARENT SPEAK

The NINE WARNING SIGNS Your Son or Daughter may be Shoplifting

1. You find merchandise price tags or package wrappings hidden in the trash.

2. You notice your child wearing new clothes, jewelry or they possesses other items that you know he or she not have the money to buy.

3. Goods show up in your child's room that you do not remember purchasing.

4. Your child lies about where new items came from ("I borrowed it from a friend").

5. Your child leaves the house with an empty backpack or large purse and/or is wearing baggy clothes or puts on a jacket when it's warm outside.

6. Your child gives expensive gifts to friends or acquaintances.

7. Your child becomes secretive about extra income they get.

8. Your child develops secretive habits during certain times of the day.

9. Money and/or property begin to disappear from family members.

Primary Sources: San Diego Police Department, Burbank Police Department (IL)

As if it wasn't hard enough being a teen, you probably don't have enough money to buy all the things you want, and you probably have no way of getting it.

This isn't true of everyone. Maybe you have classmates whose parents are way "cooler" than yours; they buy them everything they want. Suddenly you're the only one among your friends who doesn't have the latest fashion accessory or hottest gadget.

Even if they didn't mean to, your peers have put pressure on you to get the thing you want, no matter what it takes. When you don't have the money, your options are limited.

But if you shoplift to get the thing you want, what happens the next time, when something else is the latest craze and once again you're stuck without the moohlah?

THE BASICS

covet
v. to desire wrongfully, inordinately, or without due regard for the rights of others: to covet another's property.
to wish for, esp. eagerly: He won the prize they all coveted.

Definition from dictionary.com

Smile For the Camera (Why Stealing Isn't

FOOD FOR THOUGHT

Studies have shown that most kids who steal don't do it because of financial need or desire, but because of peer pressure.

A side from the fact that it's difficult to stop once you've start shoplifting and have gotten away with it (so far), the other danger you're running is a criminal record.

Thanks right. In adults, shoplifting is "commercial burglary" and is a misdemeanor. Juveniles have it slightly better. If caught, it counts as an act of delinquency. Most store owners have equipped their stores with cameras that, capture just about everything. If a store merchant suspects you of shoplifting, he or she also has certain powers of arrest. They have the right to detain you until the cops get there. Talk about embarrassing.

It doesn't matter if you're alone in your crime, or if you're caught with the friend who egged you on. There are plenty of criminal records to go around.

I was wearing a big coat with lots of pockets and had stuffed a whole bunch of stuff in them. When I walked out the door I thought I was so much smarter than everybody who spent their money on candy and stuff, until security stopped me and called the police. I was so embarrassed I thought I was going to die.

Vorth It)

PARENT SPEAK

Why Children Steal and Your Role in Preventing Retail Theft

Very young children sometimes take things they want without understanding why it's wrong. Elementary school-aged children know better, but may lack enough self-control to stop themselves. Most preteens and teens shoplift as a result of social and personal pressure in their lives. Here are just a few of the reasons why:

✓ Feel peer pressure to shoplift

✓ Low self-esteem

✓ A cry for help or attention

✓ The naïve assumption they won't get caught

✓ The belief that teen stealing is "not a big deal"

✓ Inability to handle temptation when faced with things they want

✓ The thrill involved

✓ Defiance or rebelliousness

✓ Not knowing how to work through feelings of anger, frustration, etc.

✓ Misconception that stores can afford the losses

✓ The desire to have the things that will get them "in" with a certain group of kids

✓ To support a drug habit

✓ To prove themselves to members of a gang

SOURCE: StopYourKidsFromShoplifting.com

Not Hot (How to Talk Your Friends Out of It)

PARENT SPEAK

Combating peer pressure takes a lot of courage and is not something your children will arm themselves against overnight. It is the result of years of cultivation and support from loving parents and caregivers. Only those fortunate kids who have learned respect for themselves and others and have the self-confidence and self-awareness to stand up to persuasive and often bullying pressures, survive.

To some people, shoplifting isn't about the actual object being stolen. It's about the thrill of the risk. It's about the attention and admiration of peers.

If you're with a friend and he or she announces intentions to steal something, you may be exerting a sort of peer pressure just by standing there. He or she may think that they're impressing or shocking you.

It's crucial in this situation to take the wind out of their sails immediately. Don't be afraid to be mean about it.

"What, you think you're gonna be all cool? Don't be lame. Let's go look somewhere else."

" It was all that stuff about taking your parents' car when you're 13, sneaking booze into rock shows and ditching school with your friends. I could relate to that as a former teenager, rather than as a present parent. "

—Donal Logue

You may be sparing them the trouble of a criminal record, and yourself the trouble of trying to convince the cops that you weren't an accomplice to the crime.

"The "rush" from shoplifting itself can be addictive, and people who feel the need to steal compulsively to feel that adrenaline kick are called kleptomaniacs. No matter how successful or respectable their career is, kleptomaniacs compulsively shoplift and steal, usually taking things they don't even want or need and constantly run the risk of being caught, defamed and publicly humiliated. Save yourself the trouble, just don't steal!"

WHAT DO YOU DO?

You see your friend eyeing a ring as you're shopping at Icing, and then later, when you walk out of the store together, you notice it on her finger. You're pretty sure she didn't pay for it. "Let's go in there!" she says, pointing to Claire's Accessories. Do you say something?

I have a good friend who shoplifts, and I'm always worried that she'll get caught and I'll get in trouble because I'm with her. I told her how I feel, but she keeps doing it. So, I found someone else to go shopping with.

Gotta Have It? Not That Badly! (Why anc

DR. LISA SAYS...

Before you stick that item in your pocket, just take a few seconds to think. What is the very worst thing that can happen here? Will you get caught? Will you have to go to jail? Will your parents have to leave work and pick you up from the police station? Now pretend that those things WILL automatically happen the minute that thing goes in your pocket. If you had those powers of prediction, what would you say to your friends? Now, make those words come out of your mouth and walk away.

If the urge to shoplift strikes as you're staring at that item you desperately want, ask yourself:

✎ Sure I want it now, but will I want it an hour from now? Or a week from now?

✎ Will people really be impressed if I steal this? Or will they tell me I'm cool, then talk behind my back?

✎ Can I trust all my "friends?" Will someone turn me into the authorities for this?

✎ Is it worth the risk of getting a criminal record?

If it's your friends who are egging you on with a chorus of, "Do it. Just do it. C'mon!" ask yourself:

✎ Would they admit to telling me to do it if I end up having to explain myself to cops?

✎ Hey! Why aren't they doing it?

ow You Can Resist)

PARENT SPEAK

What's Causing the Problem?

A lot of parents and teachers are perplexed by student truancy and believe it can be remedied if the students would just show up to class. However, there are a variety of reasons students stay away from school, and many of these reasons have to do with how the students feels about themselves, or their confidence in the classroom. A few of these reasons are:

✓ Feeling overwhelmed by schoolwork or personal relationships

✓ A fear of admitting failure and/or asking for help

✓ Being bullied at school

✓ Fear of safety either at school or getting to school

✓ Problems at home that make school seem irrelevant or overwhelming

The pressure to ditch is intense. Everything in school is intense. And some people act like you have to choose between their friendship and doing what you think you should be doing. I wish I had a solution.

AWOL – Ditching School

> "True terror is to wake up one morning and discover that your high school class is running the country."
>
> —Kurt Vonnegut

"I'm skipping school after lunch! Don't try to come with me. It'll be more fun if I do it alone."

That's something you'll probably never hear anyone say, ever. Ditching is typically a group activity, and for that reason you'll probably get pressured to ditch school several times before you graduate from school.

If you talk to people who routinely skip school, they'll almost never be able to tell you a good reason for having done it. "I wanted to see a movie," they might say, or "I didn't want to take the biology test."

THE BASICS

truancy
n. the act or condition of being absent without permission; failure to attend (especially school)

Definition from dictionary.com

Follow this logic for a second: You go to school to learn. If you don't learn, you'll end up dumber than everyone else. If you ditch school, you won't learn.

Ditching is dumb. Are you?

If you think you're not missing much when you ditch class, think again. And if you think your teacher isn't going to miss you when you skip, think again. And if you think that your teacher isn't going to report you absent from the class, think again. If you think there is no consequence for ditching, think again!

FOOD FOR THOUGHT

Recent studies revealed that over 60% of high school students think that school is boring. Could this be at the heart of high truancy rates?

"It's the same thing, every day. I've been going to school my whole life."

Double Trouble (Who Ditches, And Why They

Every day, hundreds of thousands of students are absent from school without valid excuses. In some schools, especially in poorer neighborhoods, truancy is such a big problem that 30% of all students can be absent on any given day. It's a serious issue that cripples our country's educational system.

So who ditches, and why? Surveys show that kids ditch school because of boredom, academic troubles, and poor relationships with their teachers.

"To wish you were someone else is to waste the person you are."

—Unknown

Vant You To Do It Too)

These are not valid excuses for being absent, and ditchers know it. That's why they may try to convince others (maybe even you) to ditch along with them. They're hoping that if you both get caught, the punishment will be lighter, both from school administrators and their own parents. They may be nervous about ditching, and may be using you for support.

The bottom line is, they don't have your best interest in mind. Why let yourself be influenced by them?

PARENT SPEAK

Self-esteem and the lack of self-esteem are qualities that are developed over time, not inherent ones. The first and foremost place that a child develops a sense of self-esteem is at home. Families who consciously seek ways to develop and encourage self-esteem as they raise their children tend to raise children who are self-aware and self-confident.

"Sometimes school is so boring, and we just can't wait to get out of there. It really doesn't matter where we go or what we do, as long as it isn't school."

Fun, But Wrong (Why You Shouldn't)

FOOD FOR THOUGHT

Bullying was reported as more prevalent among males than females and occurred with greater frequency among middle school-aged youth than high school-aged youth. For males, both physical and verbal bullying was common, while for females, verbal bullying and rumors were more common.

Source: Bullying Behaviors Among US Youth, Journal of the American Medical Association

When you're facing another boring day at school, just about everything else can sound SO much more fun.

But before you take the bait and join a bunch of your friends off campus, consider who you're hurting. Think about what you might be missing in class that might come up in an exam soon. Think about how you'd explain yourself to your parents if they found out. Think about what the truancy will look like on your school record, which, by the way, colleges will see.

The problem with truancy is that after you do it once, you won't see the harm in doing it again, and soon you'll find yourself missing more days of school than you're proud of. Did you know that 82% of convicted criminals are school drop outs? Something to think about, isn't it?

DR. LISA SAYS...

What Do You Do?
If the person you like asks you to ditch school to catch a movie, don't give in so easily. We are attracted to people who have confidence, are willing to stand up for themselves, and (yes, I hate to admit it) who play a little bit hard to get. If this person really does like you, he or she will still like you even if you can't hang out right now and need to wait until after school. Don't start out a relationship by immediately falling into a pattern of always giving in to what the other person wants, especially if what he or she wants is not good for you. Why don't you deserve to be with someone who will respect your right to get an education?

"One of the most dramatic and frequent problems we deal with at school is emotional bullying of students—usually done by leveraging friendships within a clique. One day, person A is on the outs with the group, and the next day she's back in again and person B is out. It's very painful for the kids involved."

—Ms. Jarvik, 10th grade counselor

School is Cool (No, Really. It is!)

School may bore you out of your mind sometimes, and taking exams for hours may not exactly fit your idea of a good time. But when the alternative is ditching, school may actually be the cooler choice. Here's why:

School is a controlled environment with experienced supervisors who make it their duty to keep you out of trouble. What you get when you spend your days wandering

FOOD FOR THOUGHT

Healthy friendships can contribute a lot to your school life, from giving you someone to hang out with and talk to, to actually reducing stress—yes, really. But not all friendships are healthy. A good friendship is one in which there is give and take: no one person is in control, and there is genuine care, respect and trust for each other. How do your friendships rate?

> "Don't walk in front of me, I may not follow. Don't walk behind me, I may not lead. Just walk beside me and be my friend."
>
> —Albert Camus

around outside of school is considerably less predictable.

You may fall in with the wrong crowd. You may be exposed to violence and drugs while you're wandering around, and if something terrible happens to you, no one will know where to find you. After all, they all thought you were in school! Plus, there's a direct correlation between truancy rates and daytime crime rates. Is that something you want to be a part of?

EXCUSES, EXCUSES

Keeping it Real, Keeping your Cool
If one of your friends is trying to convince you to ditch with him/her, you can always say: "When Mr. ___(insert teacher's name here)___ starts talking I totally zone out. I don't need to ditch to be not totally there, you know what I'm saying?"

> "There's so much drama with my school friends. We're always fighting about something. It's very different with my best friend. I can tell her anything and she totally understands."

ID – Being Yourself

There's Nothing Wrong With You (Being Prou

My Dad put his foot down and said 'enough' about my fighting in school. Either I had to stop hanging out with that group or he was going to take me out of school. It probably would have been easier to change schools.

You know what's best for you, and that's the truth. You have your principals, your own style, your own opinions and preferences, and if you lose any of these things to peer pressure, you lose a piece of yourself.

So what if you don't always wear or say the right things? So what if people disagree with you, or if your choices make you unpopular. Guess what? You can't put "homecoming queen" on your future resume. And for the most part, what happens in high school or junior high stays in high school or junior high. Your major embarrassments moments and social faux pas have no bearing on your future success.

PARENT SPEAK

At times, your student will have to make the very difficult decision to separate from a friend or group of friends because of a split in values or goals—or perhaps the decision will be made for them. Either way, it's a painful process and one that should be treated with the utmost care, compassion and respect.

f Who You Are)

When it comes to peer pressure, be above it. Your instinct is a better gauge of what's right for you than the opinions of your peers will ever be.

If you just stick to who you are, and do the things you like to do, you will be much happier and less stressed about trying to fit in and be cool. Let who you are shine and people will take notice and it will inspire others to be themselves. Everyone respects and admires self-confidence.

He who has a thousand friends has not a friend to spare and he who has one enemy will meet him everywhere. *"*

—Ralph Waldo Emerson

DR. LISA SAYS...

Self-respect is an incredibly important quality. Others can see it in you, even if they can't really put their finger on what they're seeing. Self-respect comes from figuring out what beliefs and values are most important to you, and sticking to them, no matter what the situation is. If you treat yourself poorly and lose control, then you are just inviting others to walk all over you. If you have respect for yourself, you will receive it from others. You will be successful in life because people will know that they can depend on you and they cannot take advantage of you.

Haters (Dealing with Them)

Some people just can't stand it when someone disagrees with them, or doesn't bend to their will. You may know some of these people. You may even consider some of them your friends.

They may try to cut you down for disagreeing with them, or doing things differently than they're used to. They may try to ruin your reputation, or try to turn your friends against you.

FOOD FOR THOUGHT

Did you know that people who speak their mind actually have lower blood pressure than those who keep their thoughts and emotions bottled up? So, in addition to the psychic benefits of opening your mouth, there are some great health reasons to do so as well.

"Speak your mind. Don't let anyone censor you. It's the best advice. Even as a teenager, I always said what I was thinking. I wasn't afraid of what others think. You have to express yourself no matter what anyone else thinks about it."

—Fran Lebowitz

These people are haters, and as annoying as they are, remember that if they have to bring you down in order to feel better about themselves, they must have some serious insecurities to deal with.

How do you deal with haters? Ignore them. Pity them, but don't let them affect you. They're not worth it.

DR. LISA SAYS...

Here is a good strategy for staying true to yourself:
Think of a few people that you really respect – family members, coaches, or teachers. Now pretend they all just walked in. How would you want to act now? What would you want them to see? You can also pretend your little sister, cousin, or the kid you tutor is watching you. What behavior would you want them to copy from you? If you wouldn't want a loved one to see you doing something or to follow in your footsteps, you should probably stop it.

I wish I could think on my feet better. I always come up with the best things to say at 11 pm, once I'm home and in bed.

BFFs (Real Friends Don't Pressure You t

Your friends should like you for who you are... not because you always agree with them or go along with their wants or wishes.

A real friend will respect you, even if they don't understand your unique style.

A real friend won't pressure you to do something you're uncomfortable with unless it truly is for your own good.

FOOD FOR THOUGHT

60 percent of boys

who were bullys

in middle school

had at least one

criminal conviction

by age 24.

(Olweus, 1993)

"Forget GPAs and SATs. Resisting peer pressure is quite often the hardest thing we ask our students to do."

——Ms. Lindstrom, 8th grade Spanish

hange)

Your true friends stand by you when the world turns its back on you.

A friend doesn't care if you're popular or un-popular... a social butterfly or a pariah.

You know in your heart who your true friends are. Treat all others accordingly.

Your true friends stand by you when the world turns its back on you.

A friend doesn't care if you're popular or un-popular... a social butterfly or a pariah.

F.Y.I.

You have friends in people you may have never met. If you're facing major social pressures and dilemmas, there are toll-free counselors who can lend an ear. Try the Boys Town National Hotline: 1-800-448-3000.

"I'm often asked if I feel proud of something I did. But what about feeling proud of who you've become?"

Walking Away–When You've

Some people just don't get the message. You can say over and over again that you're not comfortable with the way they're pressuring you. You may make your opinion perfectly clear, and they're still in your face, trying to convince you you're wrong. They're laying it on thick, trying every trick in the book to get you to do what they want you to do.

Part of having self esteem is setting healthy boundaries for yourself. If your boundaries are crossed you need to have the self confidence to let someone know. You don't have to be aggressive or angry with that person, but you should be assertive and let them not you're not O.K. with the way you are being treated. If you show people that you won't deal with them when they cross your boundaries they will respect you. Boundaries are part of your health self-respect.

When you've tried everything, and your stance is still not being respected, there may come a time when you'll simply have to walk away. This may mean stepping back from a friendship for a while, or letting it go completely.

WHAT DO YOU DO?

Your friend tells you that he/she won't be your friend anymore if you don't help him/her beat up a classmate that has offended him/her.

You want to back up your friend, but you definitely don't want a criminal record.

Tried Everything Else

It's a difficult thing to do, but sometimes it's the only way to remove the pressure.

You get enough pressure from your parents, teachers, and yourself. When it's negative, who needs it from peers, anyway?

FOOD FOR THOUGHT

71% of high school students admit to having cheated on an exam at least once. If you have never cheated, some serious congratulations are in order. You're succeeding where so many others have failed.

DR. LISA SAYS...

People are more likely to speak up when just one other person does so, even if the entire group seems to be acting as one. You are, most likely, not the only person in the group with reservations about what is going on. If you speak up, you will encourage others to do the same. You may be surprised about who ends up by your side. In the group, your questions about what the group is doing and your refusal to go along with it will probably be a great relief to at least one other person who will be quite grateful to you.

Loud (Speaking Your Peace)

DR. LISA SAYS...

Being a good friend does not have to mean that your friends are always happy with you. Do you remember a time when your parents prevented you from doing something and you were really angry about it? Then later (maybe much later...), you realized that they were right? Being a good friend is sometimes like being a good parent. If you try to talk friends out of some harmful behaviors, they may be upset with you right now, but they will eventually see that you are a moral person who can be trusted to do the right thing.

Some people are not only disrespectful of your opinion and your comfort, but they are downright insulting.

Your peers can react strongly to your resistance to their influence. They can take things personally, or take things too far. They can threaten to spread rumors about you, threaten to turn your friends against you, or threaten to hurt you with physical violence.

"From now on, I'll connect the dots my own way."

—Bill Watterson,
Calvin & Hobbes

You don't have to let yourself become a victim, just because you're standing by your principles. Speak up. Say exactly what you think of that person's attempts to pressure you and cut you down. Make sure there are witnesses. If threats are thrown around, alert school officials, your parents, or even their parents.

In not letting others control you, don't forget how much control you have over your own life. Your words have power; use them.

FOOD FOR THOUGHT

Don't get sucked into someone else's arguments. The purpose of an argument is to manipulate you into losing. If you don't get sucked in there is no argument to win, and you come out looking the better person.

(stevenaitchison. co.uk)

F.Y.I.

Most teens are susceptible to peer pressure because their friends are very important to them, and because they aren't sure of who they are yet and look to their friends as a guide.

Decide who you are and what's important to you, and you become infinitely less susceptible to pressure from your peers, friends or not.

Proud (Feeling Good About)

FOOD FOR THOUGHT

To boost your self esteem, take appropriate credit for the things you do. Don't just write off your success as "luck" or "chance." Give yourself the recognition you deserve.

True: peer pressure is all around you, and you have to face it every day. Even if you don't think you feel pressured, try to be aware of who affects your decision making. It's a basic part of life as a teen (and actually, the life of a grown up as well—although it's talked about less at that point). Even when you feel like the world is against you and that your opinion, your style, or your decisions are extremely unpopular, you have the strength to STAND UP to it. When you learn

F.Y.I.

Here's a quick checklist to run through in your head when faced with peer pressure. Consider it your crash course in dealing with it.

Think about what a group or your friends are pressuring you to do.

1) is it illegal?
2) Will it hurt someone else?
3) Is the only thing at risk your reputation?
4) What's the worse thing that can happen if you don't go along with everyone else, really?

the skills that allow you to face peer pressure head-on, you'll discover that you can be yourself and be proud of who you are.

What if you want great self- esteem and want to be proud of who you are, but you just don't feel it inside? How do you become proud of who you are? The answer is simple: Take the right action. It's hard to feel good about yourself if you do nothing worth feeling good about. It all starts with action. If you do the right thing, whether that be studying hard or having to tell someone "no" at the risk of putting yourself out there, self-respect starts with action. It's as simple as that: If you want to feel good about yourself and be respected by your peers, take the right action.

DR. LISA SAYS...

Even if you do something because of peer pressure you're not proud of, it's never too late to try to make amends. You may not fix the situation completely, but you can make it better. Did you say something mean to someone in order to try to impress someone else? Go back and give an honest apology. Did you steal something from a store? Ask to talk to the manager and return the item. Get talked into ditching school? Send an email to the teacher with an apology and express a desire to make up the work. Don't be too hard on yourself, but also don't let yourself forget the feeling of guilt and regret that you have right now.

Aww...Dealing with Rejection

"It was so unfair. One day all of us were hanging out before lunch and the next day they looked at me like I was the new kid."

You don't know what you've done, but it must be something. Do you smell bad? Did you say something? Maybe. Maybe not.

You know better than anyone how fickle other teens are. Today you're BFFs, tomorrow, you couldn't be any less.

Rejection is so hard to deal with and, because humans are thinking, feeling beings, it's hard not to analyze and overanalyze a rejection, especially one that you feel is undeserved. Teens, especially, are hard on themselves.

F.Y.I.

Rejection is something that happens to everyone, no matter how smart, attractive, talented or successful. Really.

But before you let that guy or girl get to you and make you all depressed and gloomy, take a moment to look at the bright side. OK, there's no bright side, but it's not as bad as it seems right now. Tomorrow, they say, is another day.

> I take rejection as someone blowing a bugle in my ear to wake me up and get going, rather than retreat.
>
> —Sylvester Stallone

PARENT SPEAK

How do you protect your child from life's rejections? You don't. But you can provide them with some tools for dealing with it. From friendships to dating, from sports to music, from teams to college admissions, your kid is going to be rejected. It's all part of life. But they don't always know that. Help your student avoid internalizing their pain by talking with them about rejection and sharing some of your life experiences. When they hear how you, and others, have managed rejection, it'll give them some tools to combat their own.

Doh! Learning from Your Blunders

FOOD FOR THOUGHT

It's not always that bad. Sometimes you are going to say, or do, something inappropriate or offensive. Everyone has. Think about how many times your feelings have been hurt by some thoughtless words.

Maybe your rejection isn't arbitrary, but is due to something you did or a problem you caused. But before you let one stupid mistake make you feel sad and self-conscious, ask yourself how to correct your mistake and, better yet, how not to repeat it.

Ask yourself what you did wrong and why are people mad at you. Be honest. It may be easy to gloss over your own bad behavior, but no one else will be. What would you do differently next time? If you hurt another person, can you apologize and try and make it right?

"Anyone who has never made a mistake has never tried anything new."

—Albert Einstein

If your mistake is causing stresses that you don't know how to deal with, consider talking with a trusted teacher, counselor, parent, or family friend. Sometimes another person's perspective can really help.

Also, remember that time is a great healer. And sometimes there's nothing else to do but wait for the incident to blow over. It'll seem like forever, but it will blow over.

F.Y.I.

You know how everybody laughs when some guy comes out of the bathroom with toilet paper on his shoe, or when a snotty girl gets her dress stuck in her underwear? It's hideously embarrassing, but people get over it. No matter what you're feeling now, people *will* get over it.

"I was really mad because the other girls just stopped talking to me. It took a while before I realized that maybe it was my fault."

Make A Plan: Getting Clear on What You

PARENT SPEAK

Helping your student recover from rejection or another failure can be one of the most valuable lessons you ever share. Validating their frustration can be just as important. Sure, you can tell them that life will get better, because it will. But if you're able to listen to their concerns and fears, and share some of your experiences, the exchange will have a great deal more value.

So here you are, staring down rejection again. Why did it happen another time? Could you have done something differently, or better?

The answer is all in the planning. Dissect the rejection. Was it social, academic, family- or work-related? Was it arbitrary or the result of under preparation or an overzealous wagging tongue?

Plan your comeback carefully. If you missed out on getting into a club or team because you didn't qualify, then the answer is easy: practice. If it's social, it may take a bit more thinking to figure out what went wrong and how/if you can correct it.

> Life is what happens to you while you're busy making other plans.
>
> —John Lennon

Want

Think carefully and don't discount any reasonable solution—even if all seems hopeless. A few years ago, a high school senior applied to several universities and was accepted to three, but was wait listed at his first choice. His mother suggested he write a letter to the admissions board, thanking them for considering him and placing him on the wait list. How Silly, he thought, but did it anyway. Two weeks later, he was admitted. Coincidence? Probably, but he'll never know.

F.Y.I.

It might sound silly now, but eating right and getting enough sleep really do affect your moods and behavior. Try to eat some protein with your breakfast and make sure to stay hydrated so you can focus on school and not your growling stomach or parched throat.

"Don't spend your time beating yourself up over mistakes. Making mistakes is how you learn. Figure out how to do better the next time."

Never, Ever Give Up

You may bomb one test or bomb out on the practice field. You may do it again, and the time after that. Your 'funny' joke may be insulting, and your clever attempt to be cool might be seen as making fun of the wrong person. But sooner or later you'll get it right and your many attempts will have paid off and you'll get the result you want and deserve.

Don't give up if your progress isn't as speedy as you want it to be, and don't stop looking for ways to speed up your progress! Figuring out how to recover from a disadvantage is a great skill that

"Never, never, never quit!"

—Winston Churchill

takes years to perfect and will come in handy for years to come.

If life is supposed to be a journey and not just a destination, then learning how to face adversity head on is one of the parts of your life that can teach you a lot about yourself and give you many valuable lessons.

Everything you put into developing yourself now is going to travel with you to college, the workplace, and beyond. So chin up, chest out, and look ahead. And never give up.

THE BASICS

perseverance
n. Steady persistence in a course of action, a purpose, a state, etc., in spite of difficulties, obstacles, or discouragement.

Definition from dictionary.com

"You've gotta keep trying, even when it seems like failure is the only result. You can fail, but just don't give up."

Whoop, Whoop! The Victory Dance

O f course, most hard efforts don't end in failure. Most efforts reap glorious rewards. If you're working hard to overcome personal difficulties and start seeing the results, don't forget to celebrate!

As important as pushing yourself is congratulating yourself. When you know how to pat yourself on the back and allow yourself the perks of your success, you're creating your own motivation for keeping up the good work.

PARENT SPEAK

Noticing your student's successes is just as important as trying to help them through their failures. Tell your kids you're proud of them!

"The more you praise and celebrate your life, the more there is in life to celebrate."

—Oprah Winfrey

A date with the guy/girl you like? A spot on the prestigious choral group? Nice. A leisurely afternoon relaxing by the pool after the hard work is over and done with? Nicer.

Life is about balance, so work hard and play hard. Once you see the fruits of your labor, take the time to enjoy them. It will remind you what all the hard work is for and keep you motivated throughout your life.

F.Y.I.

The way to learn how to do something you want to do is to simply do it. Ask someone, take a class, practice. If you have the desire to do it, that's half the work.

> "Life has meaning only in the struggle. Triumph or defeat is in the hands of the Gods. So let us celebrate the struggle!"
>
> —Swami Sivandanda

Fighting Off What's Fighting

What Is It and How Can I Get Rid of It?

I'm so stressed," is something you've probably heard your friends say on almost a daily basis. Recently, you even find yourself chiming in with them when they complain about the mounds of homework they have or all their after school commitments. But what is stress really??

THE BASICS

stress

n. a specific response by the body to a stimulus, as fear or pain, that disturbs or interferes with the normal physiological equilibrium of an organism.

physical, mental, or emotional strain or tension: "Worry over his job and his wife's health put him under a great stress."

a situation, occurrence, or factor causing this: "The stress of being trapped in the elevator gave him a pounding headache."

You: Stress Management

Stress is the way your body reacts to demands placed on it, whether that's your upcoming advanced Algebra exam or dealing with a difficult friend. When you feel stressed by something, your body releases chemicals into your bloodstream. These chemicals can have both positive and negative effects. Sometimes stress makes you work harder to get something done, but stress can also slow you down, especially if you have no way to deal with the extra energy the chemicals produce in you.

Here, we'll help you understand the causes of stress, signs of stress, how stress affects you, and the best ways to deal with it, because when you've already got so much to do, stress is the last thing you need to worry about.

> For fast-acting relief, try slowing down. "
>
> —Lily Tomlin

FOOD FOR THOUGHT

Many studies suggest that as students get to college, their sleeping schedule suffers greatly. Lack of sleep often results in the inability to concentrate, the need for more naps, and constant fatigue. Try getting a good rest and maybe this will give you more strength to deal with school and other issues.

Whadda Mean, Take a Deep Breath?

PARENT SPEAK

No one wants to believe that they've overlooked stress overload in their son or daughter. Here are a few signs to look for:

✓ high anxiety, which can lead to panic attacks

✓ feeling pressured, hassled, and hurried all the time

✓ mood swings and irritability

✓ physical symptoms: stomach problems, headaches, chest pain

✓ allergic reaction: eczema or asthma

✓ insomnia

✓ overeating, or worse, smoking or doing drugs

✓ depression

Stress affects everybody differently. Some people express themselves as angry or frustrated when stressed, while others can become withdrawn or depressed. None of these reactions are healthy and each can come with its own set of problems. People who take their aggressions out on people around them tend to alienate friends and loved ones while those who internalize stress can develop unhealthy ways of coping, such as eating disorders or substance abuse problems. As if you weren't stressed enough, already...

Believe it or not, stress is not always a bad thing, and it's very normal. It's your body's way of reacting to any change, whether it's positive or negative. And you've probably already figured out that stress is going to be with you throughout your school career—so the sooner you learn how to manage it, the better you'll be.

One of the first things people will tell you to do is 'take a deep breath.' What does that mean, really? Simply put: Stop for a moment. Sometimes you just need to step back and get some perspective on the situation for it to begin making sense. When we're stressed, our minds and bodies have a way of taking over, making it pretty hard to think straight. What can you do to 'take a breath' and get some perspective?

✎ Get up and walk away from the computer or desk.

✎ Go for a short walk (or do whatever exercise makes you feel better).

✎ Call a friend and talk about a lot of nothing for a while.

✎ Take a short nap.

✎ Listen to your favorite music.

FOOD FOR THOUGHT

A recent study revealed that over 60% of teenagers say that they watch more than 20 hours of television per week. The main reason? For relaxation.

How Can I Quiet My Mind with All Thes

FOOD FOR THOUGHT

Students who have learned to manage stress in their daily lives report that the following five items have helped them:

✓ Making a to-do list

✓ Setting realistic goals, both short- and long-term

✓ Stopping the cycle of worrying about "what if?"

✓ Avoiding over-scheduling

✓ Turning mistakes into lessons

When stress tightens its grip on you, it seems like there's no getting away. You may feel anxious, tired, frightened or angry and might not know how to deal with these emotions.

The truth is, everyone feels this way sometimes. It's not about the stress, it's about what you do with it. Sounds silly, right? But it's true.

The best way to deal with stress is not to avoid it, which is impossible, but to learn how to work with it. Here are a few suggestions for thinking about yourself and your well-being first:

✎ Try breathing exercises.

✎ Make an effort to think positively.

✎ Make time to relax and take a break.

✎ Read something uplifting or inspirational.

✎ Use positive visualization techniques—if you see it, you can do it!

✎ Talk it out with a friend or counselor.

oices?

✎ Don't focus on the negative.

✎ Take pride in your accomplishments.

✎ Allow yourself to make some mistakes.

✎ Eat something healthy.

✎ Exercise.

✎ Find something outside of school you like to do, and do it.

✎ Make time for fun!

F.Y.I.

Use these four steps to problem solving:

1. Brainstorm solution
2. Think of the consequences
3. Choose a solution
4. Evaluate your choice

"Don't underestimate the value of doing nothing, of just going along, listening to all the things you can't hear, and not bothering."

—Pooh's Little Instruction Book, inspired by A.A. Milne

What Is It? Move or Sit Still?

Depending on your personality, different types of exercise may help you relieve stress. Yoga, which emphasizes quiet mediation, a focus on breathing, and lots of stretching and strengthening, can be great therapy for stress management.

FOOD FOR THOUGHT

A half an hour of exercise at least three times a week is an excellent way to get into shape and keep your body less tense. Start by walking around the neighborhood or maybe even enjoying a dance workout video!

"Part of being a winner is knowing when enough is enough. Sometimes you have to give up the fight and walk away, and move on to something that's more productive."

—Donald Trump

Yoga, is a non-competitive activity that gives everyone a chance to move at their own pace and focus on their own personal growth. With a competitive environment at school, yoga can give you the "breathing room" you need to deal with that stress.

Yoga is exercise that is good for the mind, body and soul and is an excellent outlet for those needing a little more quiet time in their lives. Sometimes when life is hectic, the best thing you can do is slow down and take some deep breaths.

F.Y.I.

Does Yoga seem too slow for you? Are you more into fast paced workouts? Try the new "hip" thing: Power Yoga. Power Yoga is essentially yoga with more swift and dynamic movements. It still gives your body that flexibility and ease, but also keeps you awake and refreshed!

> " I never thought I had time for exercise until I started going with my roommate. Now I can't imagine not going. "

Exercise Does Calm the Body

For those who need to move around to burn off that extra energy, a high paced cardio workout might be a better solution. Something a simple as going for a run or jumping rope can allow you to focus again.

You don't have to go to the gym to get a good workout. You can take a run in your neighborhood or hike in the local park or foothills. When you're short on time, you can take a walk, get some fresh air, and burn a little stress energy.

FOOD FOR THOUGHT

Exercise is necessary for students because of the related cognitive benefits. What does that mean? When you move your body, your brain works better. Enough said.

"There are thousands of causes for stress, and one antidote to stress is self-expression. That's what happens to me. My thoughts get off my chest."

—Garson Kanin

Like a more structured routine? Sign up for an aerobic or spinning class or try kick boxing. Not only will you work out some aggressions, you'll build up some stamina, too.

Getting into a fitness routine doesn't have to be complicated—it's supposed to take your mind off stress. Enlisting a friend or workout buddy commits you to regular workouts and the time spent with someone you enjoy has added health benefits.

Try scheduling your exercise in with your other appointments. Not only will you be more inclined to show up and get moving, you'll avoid the guilt of missed workouts.

F.Y.I

According to recent studies, more than 70 million Americans walk to work out, making it the most popular form of exercise.

"I'm really into my running workout. Running really helps me clear my head and makes me feel good, especially when I'm stressed."

—Katie Holmes

RESOURCES

Below are some great web resources for you and your parents to check out:

www.4Parents.org

www.AboveTheInfluence.com

www.TheCoolSpot.gov

www.DrDrew.com

www.Education.com

www.GirlsSpeakOut.org

www.IWannaKnow.org

www.Kaplan.com

www.KidsHealth.org

www.ParentingTeens.About.com

www.PreteenAlliance.org

www.ReachOut.com.au

www.TeenAdvice.About.com

THINGS TO THINK ABOUT

We've left you room to jot down notes of issues you want to discuss with friends, teachers or parents. We hope you use these pages as you read to personalize this book, and make it your own.

THINGS TO DO

THINGS TO DO

THINGS TO TALK TO MY
TEACHERS/PARENTS ABOUT

THINGS TO TALK TO MY TEACHERS/PARENTS ABOUT

THINGS TO TALK TO MY FRIENDS ABOUT

THINGS TO TALK TO MY FRIENDS ABOUT

JUST THINGS

JUST THINGS

JUST THINGS

Want more help dealing with the stress in your life? Look for these
other books from Kaplan Publishing. Available wherever books are sold:

SOS Guide to Dealing with Tests
(Available in September 2008)

SOS Guide to Saying No to Cheating
(Available in September 2008)

SOS Guide to Managing Your Time
(Available in March 2009)

SOS Guide to Getting Into Clubs and Sports
(Available in March 2009)

SOS Guide to Tackling Your Homework
(Available in March 2009)

Do your parents need a refresher course when it comes time
to help you or your siblings with math homework? Tell them about:

Kaplan's Math for Moms and Dads
(Available October 2008)
This primer gives them all the terms, concepts, and helpful tips
they've forgotten since high school.